A Gift from the Elementals

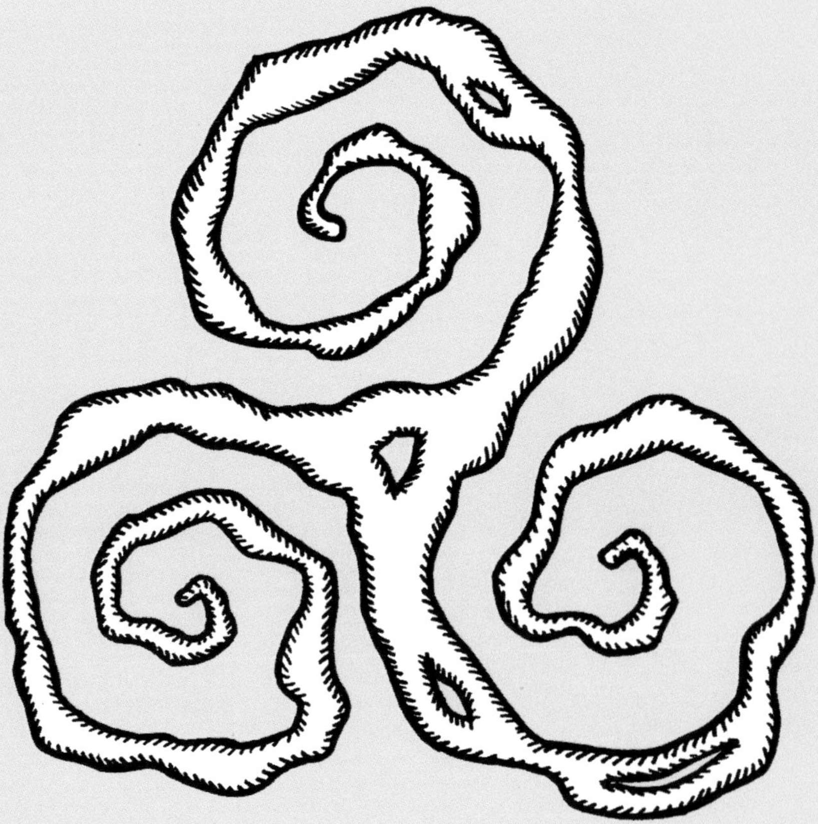

A Gift from the Elementals

by

Yvette C. Abid

Dear Susan,
Wishing you love,
health + happiness
+ everlasting life.
Yvette x

First published in 2017 by Yvette C. Abid

Published by Planet VII

Typesetting in Zapf Chancery by
Edward Sturgeon

Artwork by Hedar A. Abid
Printed in Great Britain by Print2Demand

A catalogue record of this book is available from
The British Library
ISBN 978-15272-0830-8

This book was given to me over the course of just three or four months at the beginning of 2016. When two of my children moved back to live with me at the end of 2015, I had found it difficult to find the time to meditate. I picked up pen and paper and just sat still, whereupon the words just seemed to flow, non-stop, for three months.

One particular poem, "Titania", was a light-bulb moment, when I realised these poems really had to be published. I had written "Titania" on a scrap of paper late one night, but was reluctant to put it in my manuscript book, believing people would think me ever so slightly bonkers to admit to a belief in fairies! However, I then received a message from the spirit world, channelled through the medium Lesleigh Badgery, thanking me for the work I had been doing. Lesleigh is a gifted spirit portrait artist (www.the-lantern-of-light.com) and provided the illustration of Titania (although she thought the name was Tatiana) before the clairvoyance service had even begun at my local Spiritualist Church. She had no idea of my close connection to nature and certainly hadn't a clue that I'd just written a poem about the Queen of Fairies!

Never having written poetry ever before, I suppose you could say this is my debut collection. However, I have no idea if I will be given any future volumes, so please enjoy this one while you can!

In love and light,
Yvette C. Abid

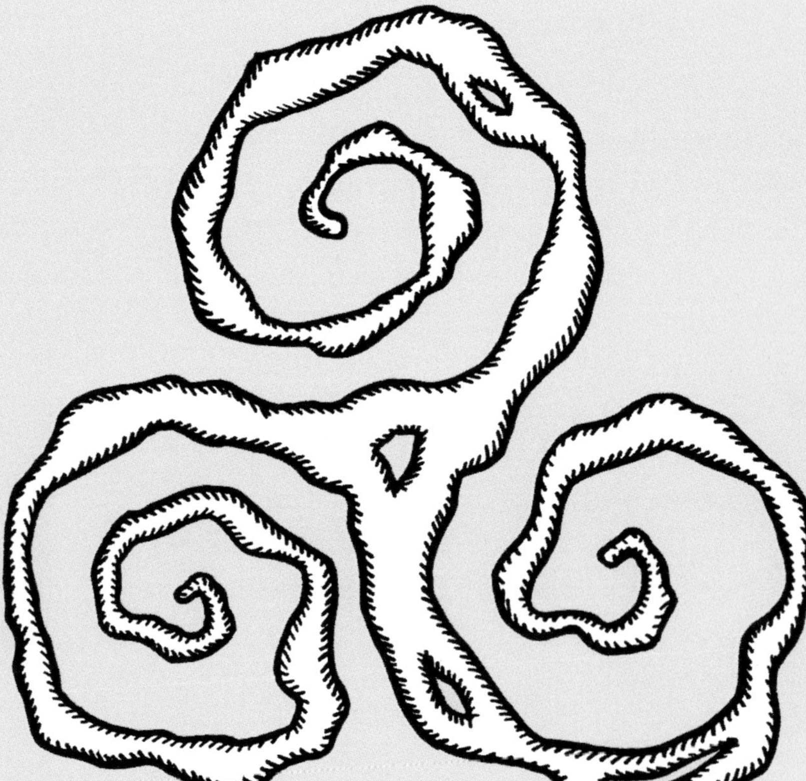

This book is dedicated to the three most important people in my life ~ Hajir, Hedar and Heval.

Thank you for the honour of being your mother.

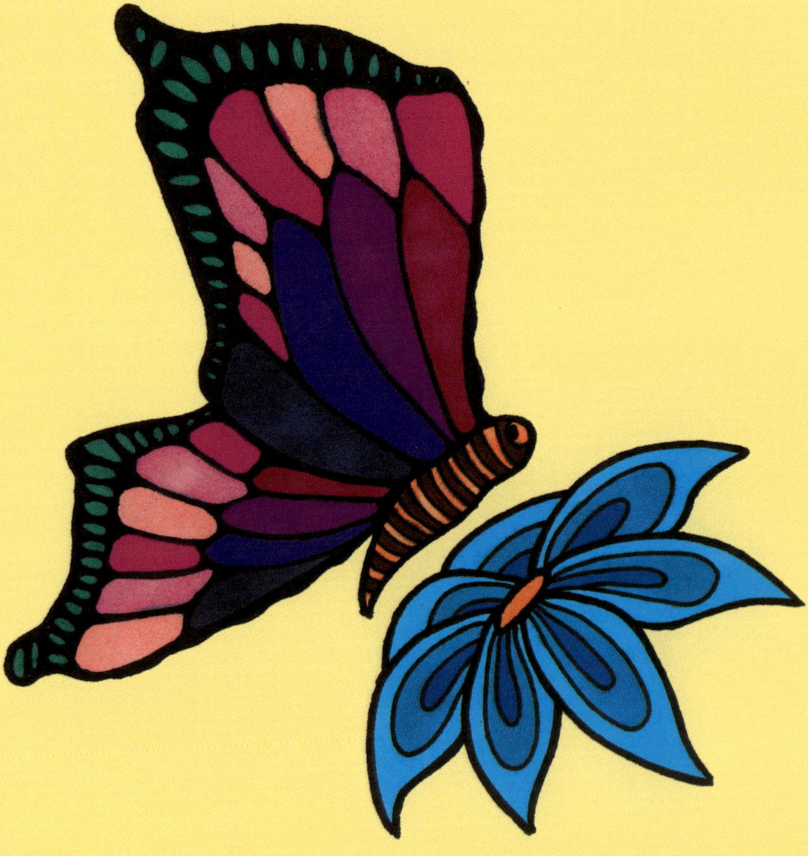

The Lightgivers' Way

Guardians and angels, please hear this prayer;
My heart and soul to you I bear.
Please help me safely through each day,
And guide me along the Lightgivers' Way.

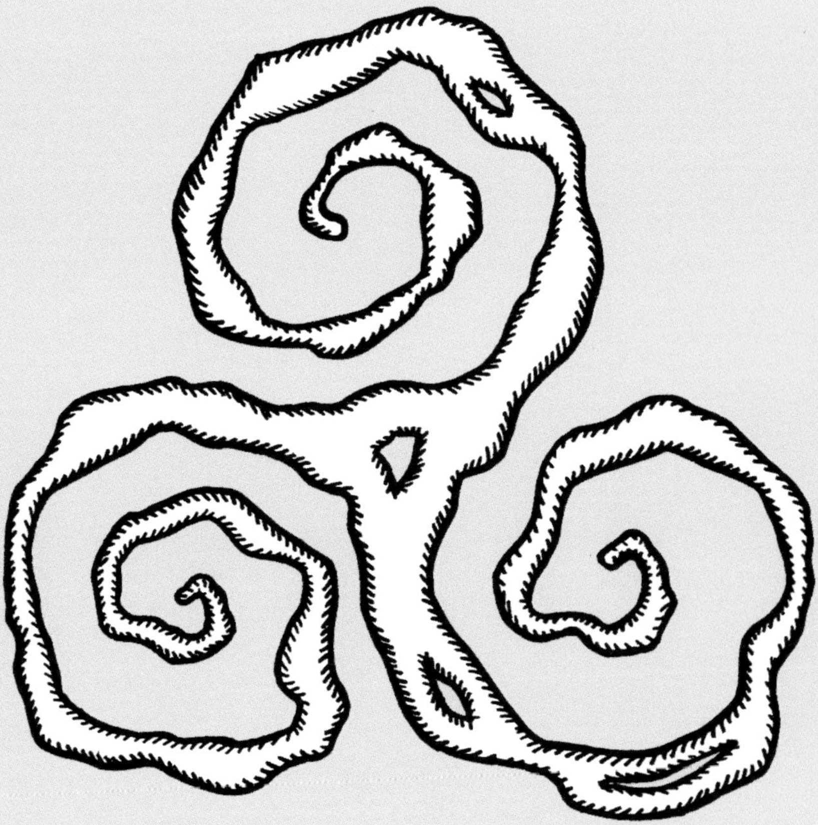

21st Century Child

Children are funny young things;
They cause us such grief whilst growing,
Yet impart to us such light and knowing.
They break the rules and delight in quarrels,
Yet astound and amaze us with their justice and morals.
They follow not the way that we show,
But just see how their auras do glow;
Twenty-four carat gold.

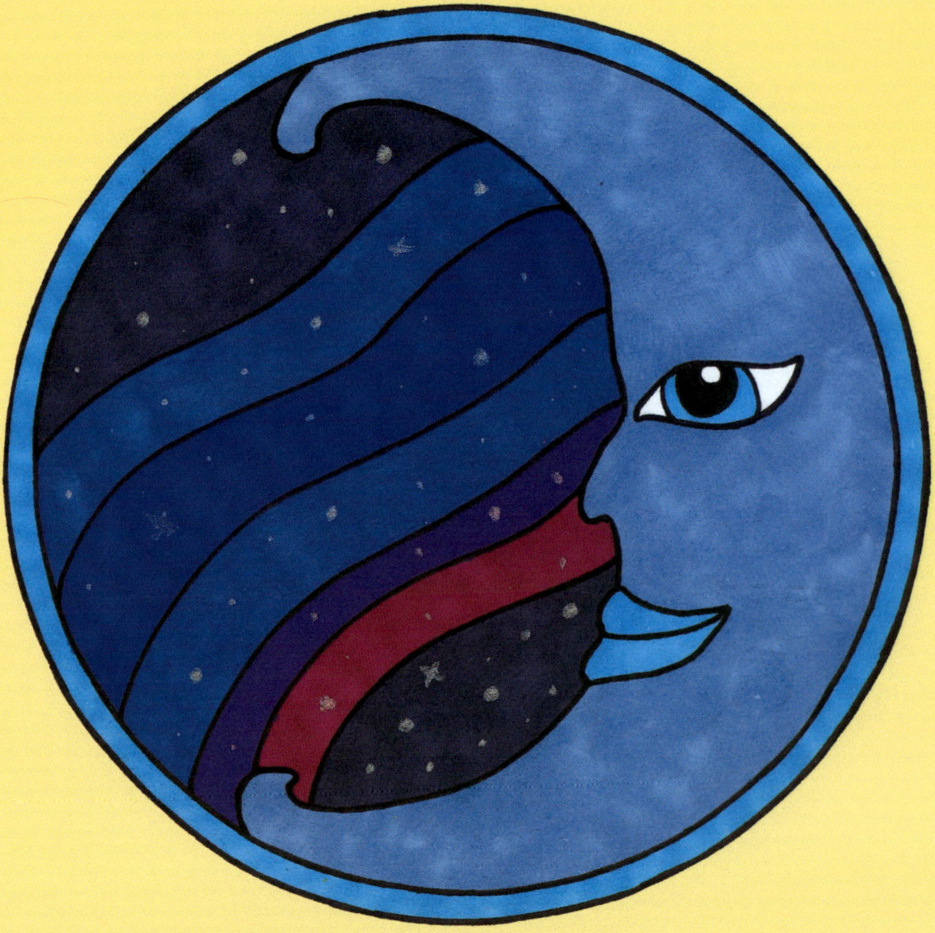

A Wonder to Behold

Praise be to Kingu, guardian of the Earth,
Whose light has watched over us since planetary birth,
Home of The Watchers, who guide us on our course,
And causation of Gaia's oceanic force.
Gleaming and opulent in the velvet sky,
Mysterious prince; our glorious Moon passes by.

Spirit in the Sky

As I sit yogic-wise,
Gazing out toward the skies,
A flock of starlings in their radiant livery,
Circle above in perfect harmony.

How do they know when it's time to turn?
How long does it take for each bird to learn?
They dance joyfully in unadulterated bliss,
Oblivious to all but the avian abyss.

Going Up

Don't sweat the small things,
For life has much to throw our way.
With health and finance, love and war,
It's hard to promise that we will stay.

But we chose this life, beloved friend,
So please stick with us until the end,
So that our souls will grow and all will know,
That we paid for our ticket to rightfully ascend.

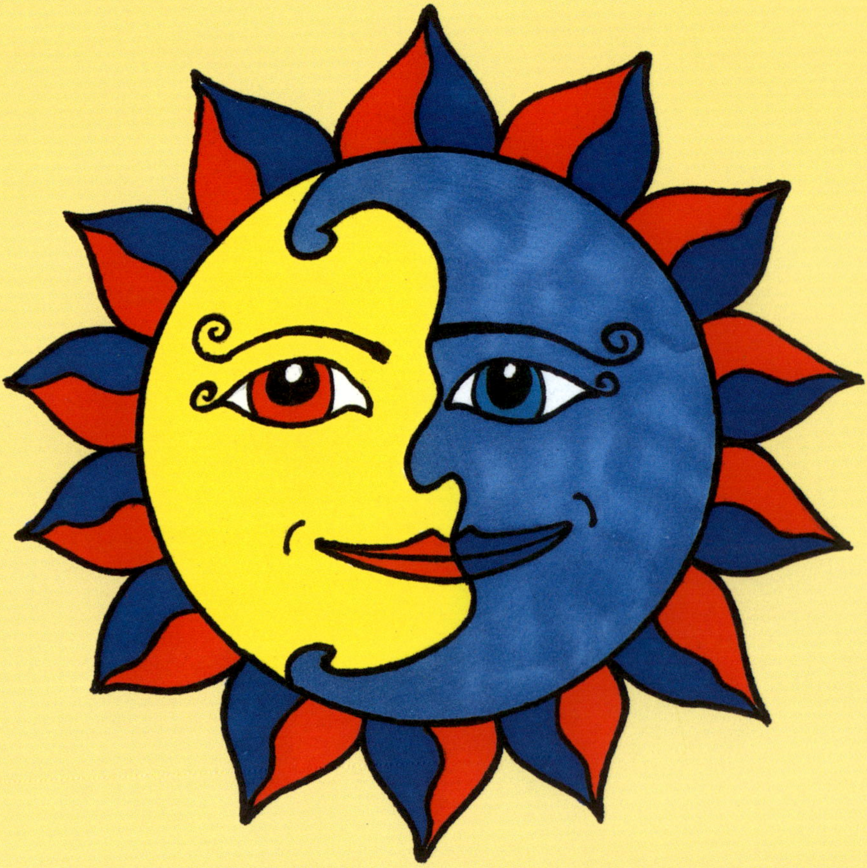

A Psalm for Solstice

Brother Sun and Sister Moon,
Rain down your golden silver light,
Upon the vast, enduring Ocean,
Surrounding this, our Earthly satellite.

Sister Moon and Brother Sun,
Send forth your magnetic rays,
To hold our Ocean in true balance,
Through diurnal and nocturnal phase.

As the solar-lunar synergy,
Embraces all upon our Earth,
Let Aphrodite and Poseidon,
Preserve the waters around her girth.

We give thanks for our life-affirming Ocean,
As we genuflect in awe and resolute devotion.

Your Pain is my Pain

Is this the price I have to pay,
For living in a place much blessed,
Where almost all the things I need,
Into my outstretched palms are pressed?

When life is good and chance of survival high,
In steps karma to reveal the lie:
Life was indeed too good to be true;
Now I know, the price was paid by you.

A Minor Inconvenience

When Earth breathes in, terra firma rents asunder,
Volcanic peaks spew forth to the echoes of fierce thunder.
She exfoliates impurities in readiness to breathe out,
To be cleansed of the poisons beyond reasonable doubt.
Inconvenient it may be to us, the mortal one,
But Earth must attune to the Universal Ohm.

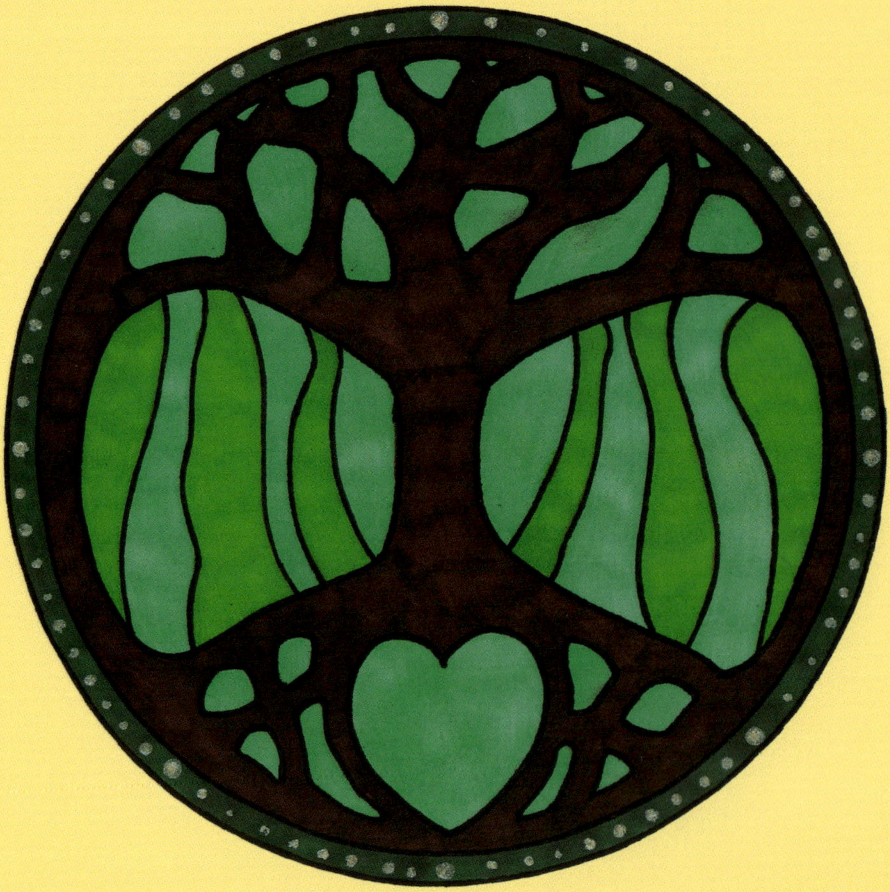

Quercus Robur

The majestic Oak stands tall and proud,
It's mighty boughs home to a motley crowd.
It shelters the minutiae of the insect mundi,
The mammals and birds from the fields just ploughed.
Strong and enduring, it protects them all,
Into its welcoming embrace the animalia crawl.

Exit Stage Left

Lost to conscious memory,
Yet accessed in dream state,
Life's trials and tribulations,
Are acting out our fate.

The loved ones lost, the friends we've crossed,
And those we love to hate;
All have roles in this Game of Souls,
Leading us back to Heaven's Gate.

Stay Close to Me

I know you are but a breath away;
They tell me each and every day.
All I need do is close my eyes,
And a vision of you is my welcome prize.

But when the cloak of grief is heavy,
And the pain of loss cuts deep,
Then it's hard to see and hear and feel;
I long for the blessed, endless sleep.

I know you are but a breath away,
And I know it's here that I must stay.
The course we chose as a pair to travel,
Now alone I must unravel.

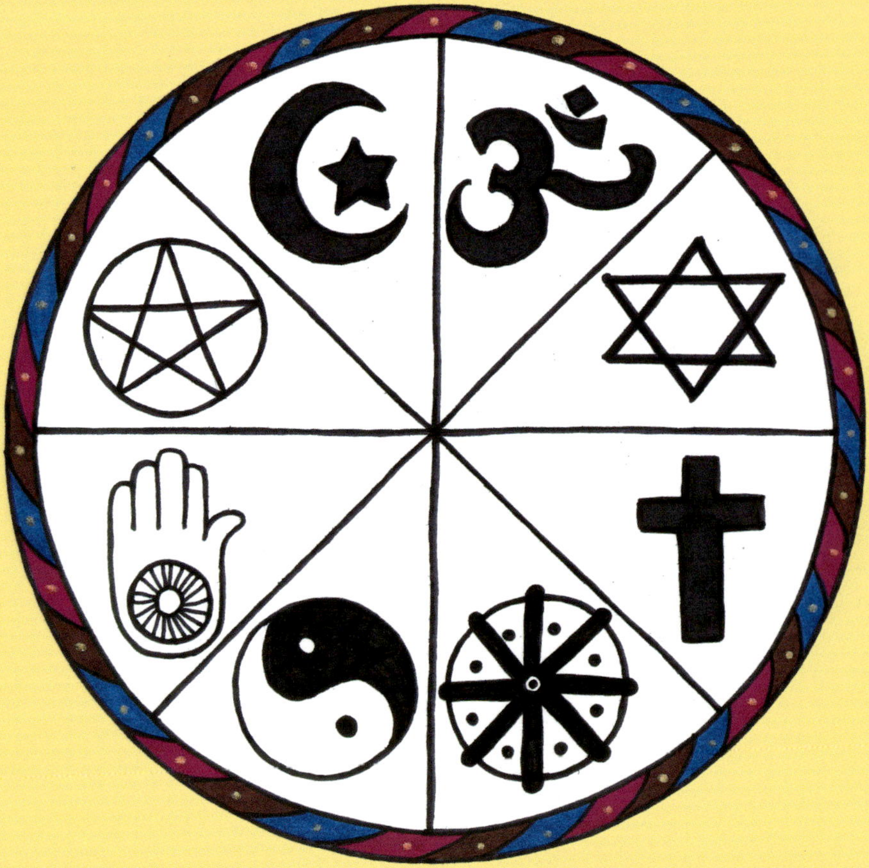

The
Liminal Zone

Occupying the space 'twixt here and there,
The adept and yogi their experiences share.

One says he knows the way to enlightenment,
The other is.

Believing is Seeing

"Mummy, can you see me?" little Lucy cried.
Mummy turned her face to Flossie, sitting by her side.
Flossie purred and stretched her back,
Then fixed her eyes in forward stare.
"You silly mog" said Mummy,
"There isn't anybody there".

But Flossie kept on staring,
And Lucy cried once more,
"Mummy, why can you not see me?"
But Mummy's heart was sore.

Lucy smiled at Flossie,
And Flossie mewed a greeting.
Mummy thought she heard a laugh;
The dawning of their spirits' meeting

Treading Water

Gliding with no visible effort upon the lake of life,
The swan is powerful and serene.

It's beauty is evident for all to see,
But it's strength is hidden below the water's sheen.

Feeling the Love

Some people are meant to see,
Some are meant to hear;
Some will think and feel and be,
Some just know when Spirit is near.

All of us are different,
Yet we all are just the same;
Striving for the betterment,
Of this, our mortal frame.

So look to the God within,
And not to the God above;
For there will your healing begin,
If you can treat yourself with love.

The Journey Home

It rained that day, when her Spirit left;
The sky was black and she felt bereft.

All joy had gone from her Earthly life,
This beloved sister, mother and wife.

But when we gathered to say goodbye,
Not a cloud was there in the sky.

Pure blue, pure energy, pure love, pure air;
Pure joy was restored, beyond compare.

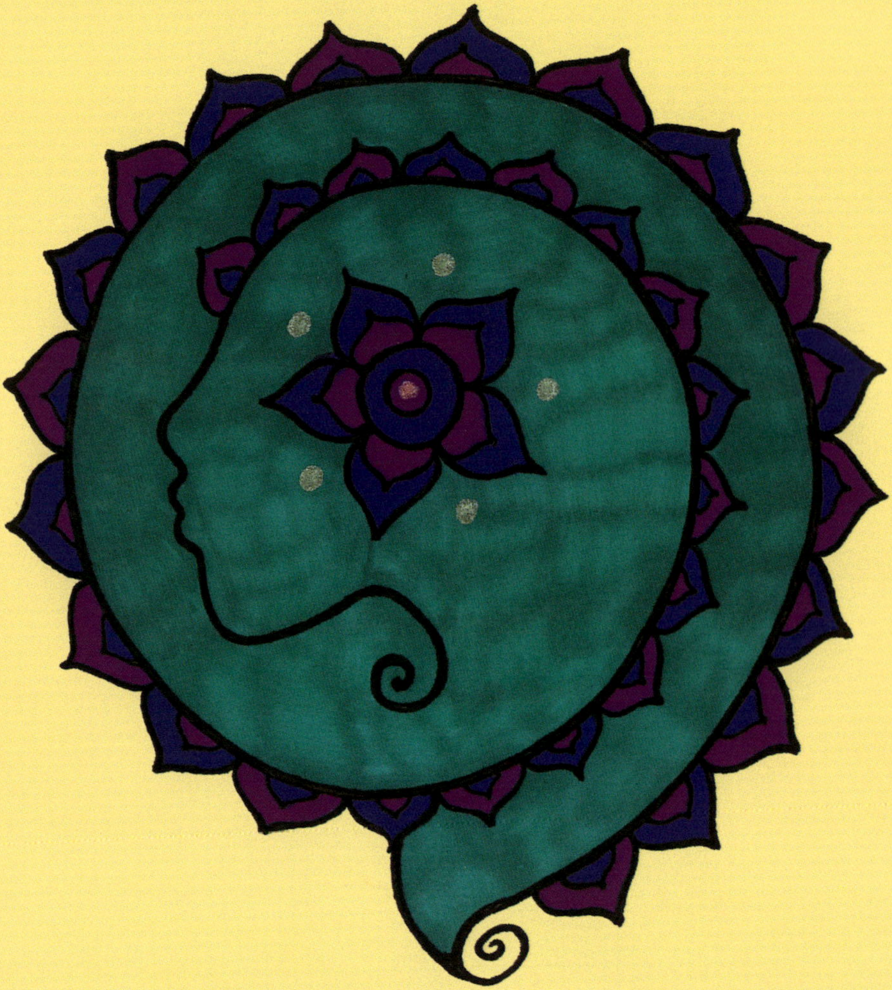

Lost in Space

Swirling through the eyes of time,
Concentric circles of violet and lime,
Spinning, revolving, evolving into space,
Twisting, stretching, vanishing without trace.

Behind closed eyes, the purple pours,
Flowing, growing, with no known cause,
Except the Self's desire to resonate higher,
And to follow the path of the Spiritual Laws.

The Sleeping Army

In the hours of our slumber,
The reveille calls us to our post;
Every man, woman and child,
Each father, son and holy ghost.

All join together for the task that lies ahead:
Gathering up the souls of the newly-departed dead.

Each night the work is harder,
Than the night that went before,
But every soul is gold-dust;
Not one can we ignore.

The work is thankless whilst on the Earthly plain,
But in Paradise, Valhalla, Nirvana or Shambhala,
The rescue of these souls will never be in vain.

The Middle

Whatever happens when we reach the helm,
That we cannot see the other realm?
In childhood our Guardians agreed to send,
A spirit light, our 'invisible friend'.
In dotage, Spirit gathers all around,
And departed loved ones again are found,
But in the long and arduous middle years,
We steer our ship through joy and tears,
Ever trusting we are not alone;
Ever mindful we must atone.

Raising the Vibration

Sitting amidst the bowls of brass,
The lama proceeds to show his class,
The resonant frequencies of each bowl,
And how they heal both heart and soul.

The bowls ring out in harmonic moans,
Piercing through to their very bones.
The monks sit motionless, frozen to the spot,
Where the tones of Solfeggio meet Mandelbrot.

"Sin" City

No-one said it would be easy,
To walk this mortal path.
No-one warned us to expect,
Such venomous and hateful wrath.

But if you can look beyond the "crook",
And see the hurt within,
You wouldn't be so quick to blame,
And call the deed a "sin".

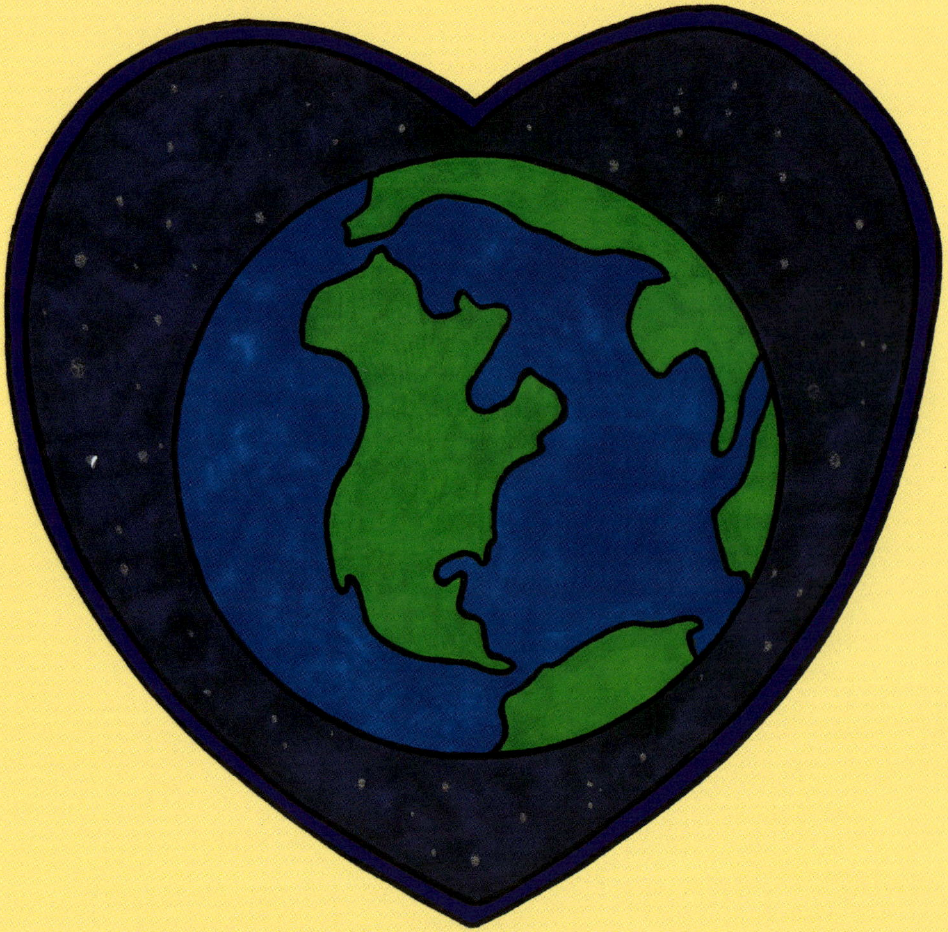

Ode to Gaia

Tread lightly on the Earth,
For she is bruised and in much pain.
She has given of her heart and bared open her soul,
All for our benefit and gain.

Her days are numbered, her life force low,
Would that it were not so,
But we two-leggeds have been greedy,
And Earth has lost her glow.

All she ever wanted was to bear us fruits and love;
Now she is ascending to the dimensions up above.

Taking One for the Team

Once upon the Rainbow Bridge,
A troubled Spirit paused,
Unsure he qualified to proceed,
Recalling the chaos he had caused.

When across the bridge from the other side,
Came the Angels to escort him,
He shied away and hid his face,
Fearing his chances to be slim.

But the Angels smiled, with outstretched arms,
And thanked him for his turn;
For without his acts of rebellion,
How could other team members learn?

Chakra Wash

*Red for the rubies and blood of survival,
Orange for carnelian and emotional revival,
Yellow is for citrine and fire in the belly,
Green for emeralds and the Venus of Botticelli,
Blue is for turquoise, creativity and sound,
Indigo for the sapphires where 3rd sight can be found,
Violet for the amethyst, knowledge and thought,
White for the diamonds and transcendence for which we have fought.*

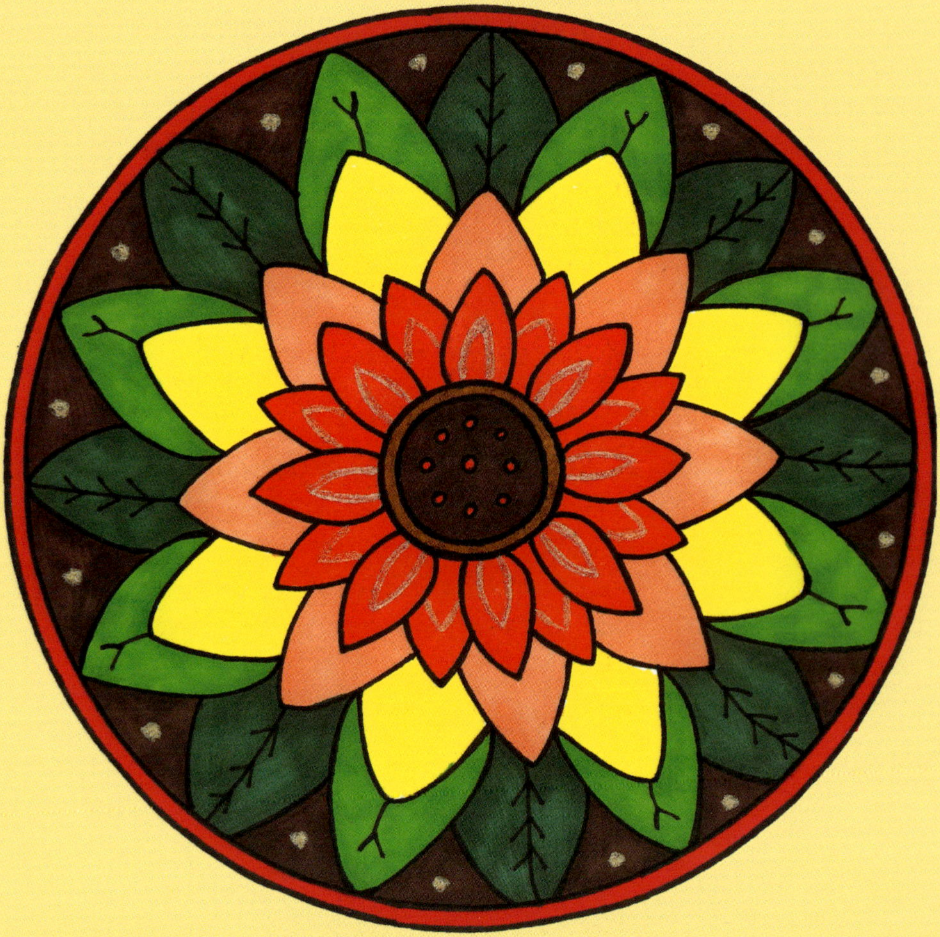

On Perseverance

Polyanthus, you make me so proud,
As each time the mower clips your leaves,
You spring back up with the herbaceous crowd,
And my heart another floral blessing receives.

Memory Lane

Watching glistening raindrops trickling down the pane,
His finger traced the way, then back to the top again.
His eyes glazed over in silent reverie,
And he smiled at another rescued memory.

The uniforms bustled all around,
And the monitors made a humming sound.
The wheels of his chair were locked into place,
As the smile expanded all over his face.

Recalling the wisdom of his departed wife,
He looked back over an eventful life:
"Raindrops precipitate, evaporate then rise".
His smile simply broadened; then he closed his eyes.

Chaos Theory Soundbite

The emerald and cobalt dragonfly,
Flexed his wings by the stream.
The dazzling reflection on the water,
Woke the heron from his daytime dream.

He stepped out to where the stream flowed faster,
Then launched himself into the air,
Startling the grazing buck rabbit,
Who bolted toward the fox in his lair.

The fox seized his chance,
And made his advance,
Never knowing his luncheon supply,
Was courtesy of the dragonfly.

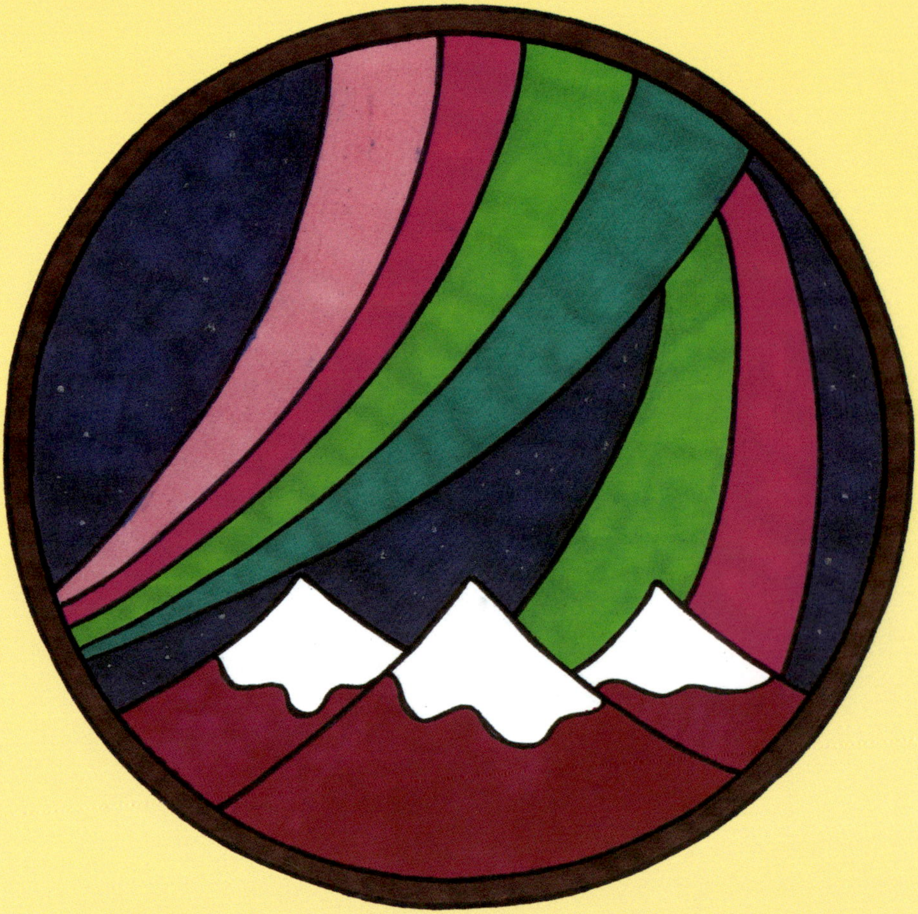

Bathed in Glory

In a place toward the Northern sky,
Where ice and snow in slumber lie,
Where night is day and day is night,
There appears above a wondrous sight.

The colours of Aurora shower down in magnetic arcs,
Gushing forth their fluorescent and multitudinous quarks.

For a few brief moments, the Earth is bathed in light,
And her aura is regenerated; vibrant, pure and bright.

Chasing the Rainbow

Speak to me of fluffy things,
Of rainbows, unicorns and light.
Keep the conversation positive,
Yes can do, upbeat and bright,
For my heart is truly breaking,
The Universe itself is aching,
As darkness seeks to obscure our sight.

Please lift my spirit with talk of peace,
Of compassion and of love;
Of sisterhood and brotherhood,
And the symbol of the dove,
For only if our thoughts are pure,
Can light the darkness then obscure.

The Feeding Station

Form an orderly queue please, for nuts and seed and fat.
For all discerning garden birds, this is where it's at.
The jackdaw contorts his bulky frame;
To dislodge the coconut is his game.
Robins, bluetits and sparrows abound,
Tipping seeds upon the ground,
Where the waddling pigeon patrols the deck,
Scooping up spillages with a nodding, rhythmic peck.

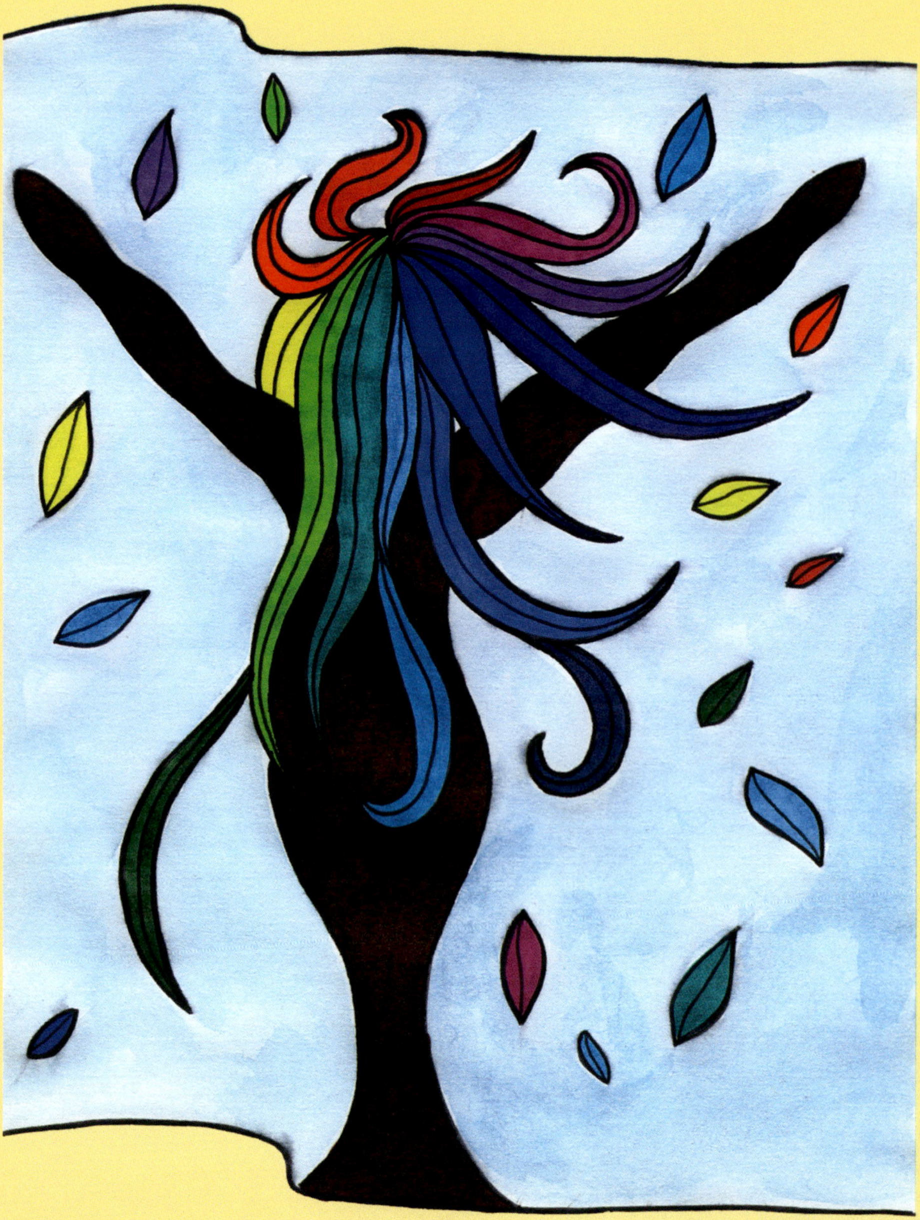

Woden's Tree

The Wisdom Tree projects a proud silhouette,
As it blows and bends on the mountainside.

Luscious, ruby-red berries aplenty;
A place of safety for the Nordic birds to hide.

Odin himself, The Hanging Man,
Once swung from its sturdy boughs.

Runic Tree, Rowan Tree,
Spirit of Sophia, in us please rouse.

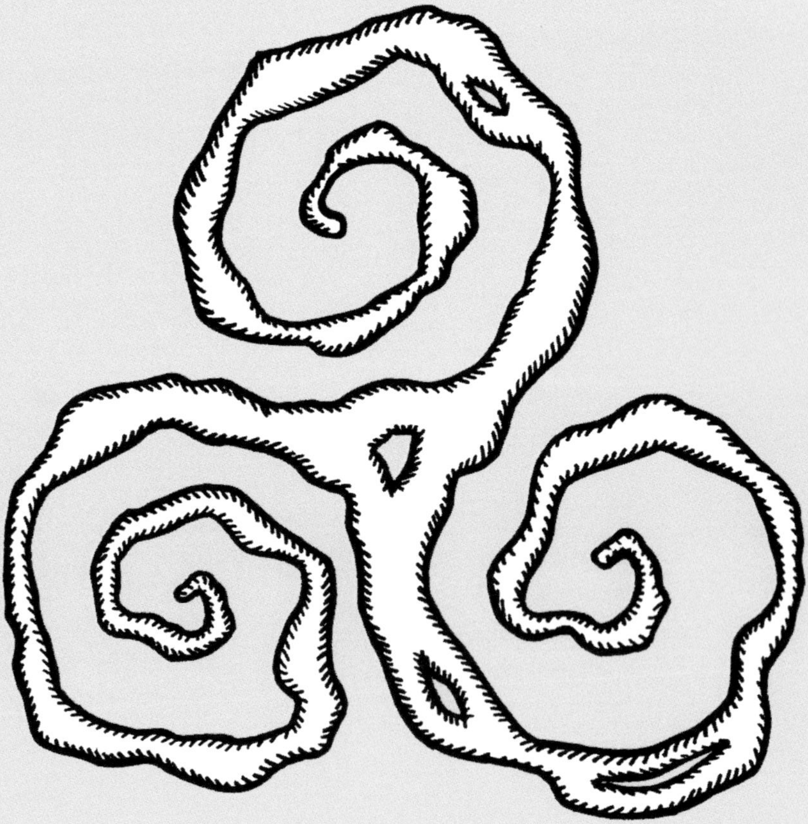

Sensory Overload

When you look upon the butterfly,
And the shimmering colours of its wings;
When you see the wildflower meadow,
The ladybirds and God's other tiny things…

When you hear the songbird's light refrain,
And the rhythmic purring of the turtle dove;
When you hear the babbling brook,
As the stream descends from the rocks above…

When you smell the perfume of the honeysuckle,
And the fragrance of rock rose;
When the aroma of sweet jasmine,
Is detected by your nose…

When you sample the gluey produce of the bees,
Their golden honey, sweet and full of flavour;
When you taste the wild fruits and berries,
Just waiting for us to pick and savour…

When you feel the weightless breeze of summer,
As it soothes and strokes your face;
When you feel the gentle softness of the grass,
The warm and cosy safeness of this place…

Then you'll know you have found something fundamental,
For this is the domain of the Earthly Elementals

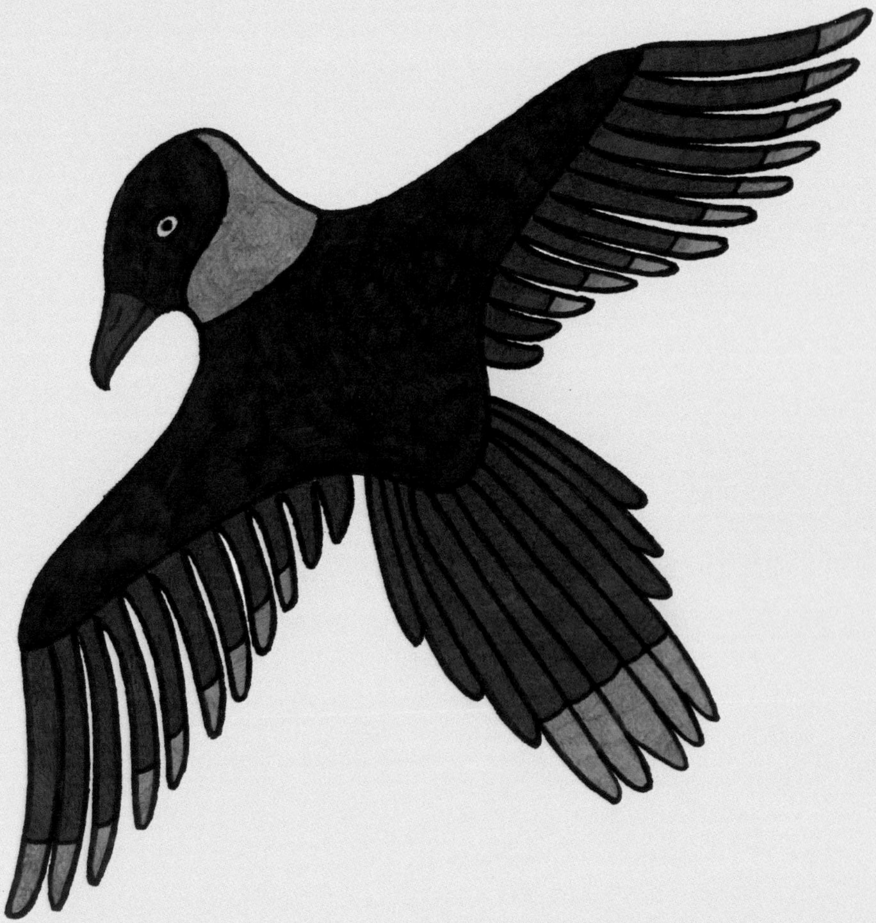

The Mob

Fear not the corvid's hood,
For they are much misunderstood.

Threads of jet, these knowing guys,
Guard their patch from predating eyes.

Their intelligence goes understated,
Their brotherhood much under-rated.

Fear not the corvid in your 'hood,
He is but a rough diamond done good.

The Triune

On a frosty, cold, midwinter night,
Keep the homefires burning bright,
In remembrance of Vesta's eternal flame,
And the maidens who to the temple came,
To serve the Goddess of hearth and home;
Praise be to maiden, mother and crone.

The Stepping Stones of Life

The friends we have today,
Won't necessarily be there tomorrow,
But those who decide to stay,
Will help us through laughter and sorrow.

Do not grieve for the friends who leave,
For their path is but their own.
Be proud to have known them,
And glad to have grown with them,
As they strive to arrive at their next stepping stone.

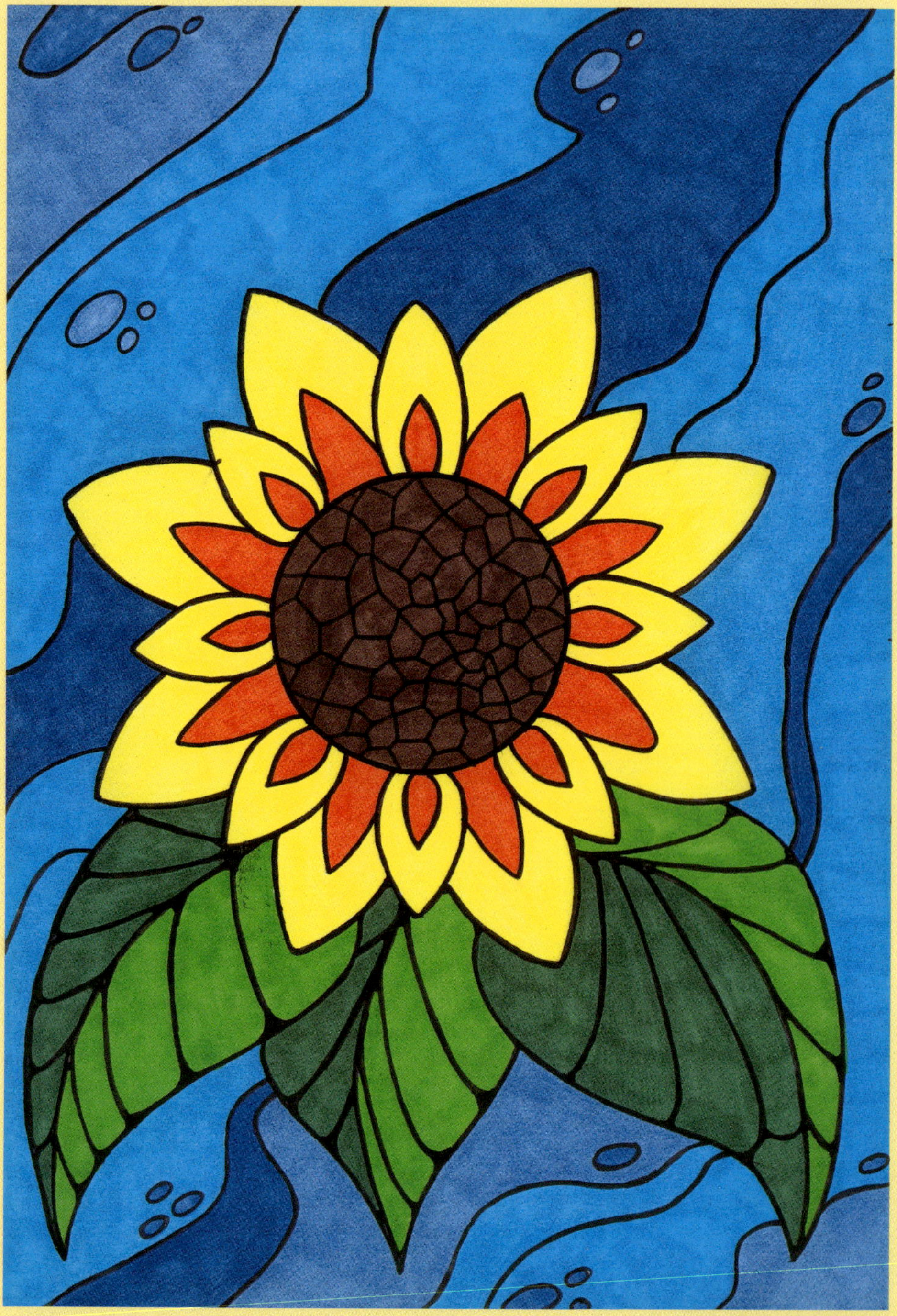

I.S.S. in Bloom

In the deepest, darkest depths of Space,
There float the most dynamic of the human race,
On a quest to discover the origins of Earth;
To ascertain the date of Universal birth,
For Man is ever curious to know,
How we are made and how things grow.

Many and complex are the tests carried out;
Can plants survive in deluge or drought?
Yet the proudest moment for our rocketeers,
Was the flowering of the golden Zinnias.
Their delicate petals gently unfurled;
The rootstock and spirit of a brave new world.

The
7th Heaven

They've travelled many light years,
To reach this destination,
Through warping of the spacetime,
And avid calculation.

Past Pluto, Neptune, Uranus and Saturn,
To Jupiter ~ avoiding belted asteroids to learn.
Then loomed Mars, the harbinger of war;
They have been there many times before…

On Planet Seven, we search the skies,
Ancient prophesies to realise.
We know the travellers will reappear,
In the Age of Aquarius ~ but in which year?

Rosslyn

Solomon's ancient blueprint,
Lies on Caledonia's eastern shore,
Concealing Templar mysteries,
And esoteric lore.

Within its Masonic framework,
Are treasures of eternal worth,
Where Green Man meets Holy Grail,
Creating heaven here on Earth.

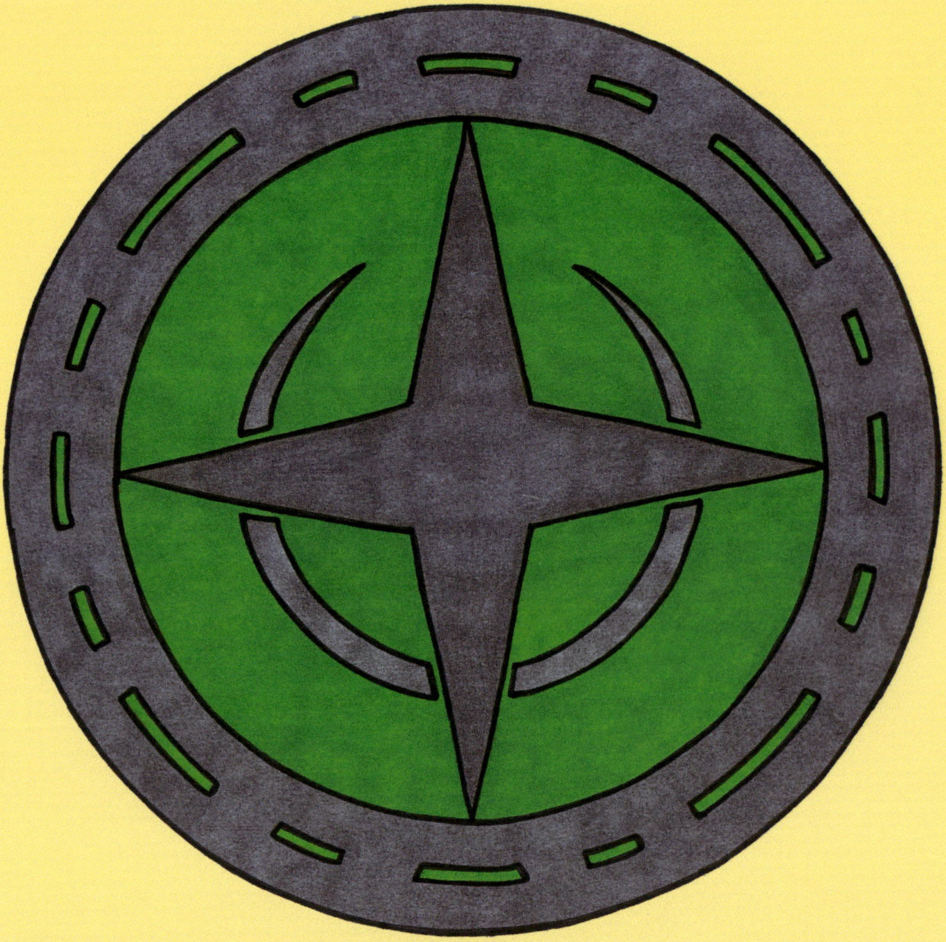

Signs of the Times

Mandala-like, the circles form,
With messages of our fate.
Year on year, the corn is torn,
To warn our time is getting late.

Cycles of the Universe and cosmic cataclysms,
Squaring of the circle and geometry of prisms;
All are revealed in the field.
We have but to decipher the cereals' yield.

Fate
or Fortune

"So you have free will" He said,
(I imagined I could do as I please).
"But with free will comes responsibility",
(I'm responsible ~ this will be a breeze)!

But He said nothing of the inequality of life on Earth,
Whilst advising we could choose our own circumstance of birth.

I picked The West ~ it was luscious and green.
Some chose The East ~ its fate not clearly seen.
What vagaries decide who lives and who dies?
That responsibility with all of us lies.

Paws for Thought

Don't give me that hang-dog look;
There's no time today for walkies.

I'll make it up to you tomorrow;
And no, I'm not just telling porkies!

But then you were a poorly pooch,
And tomorrow never came.

I'm so sorry we didn't walk out more,
And play one last round of your favourite game.

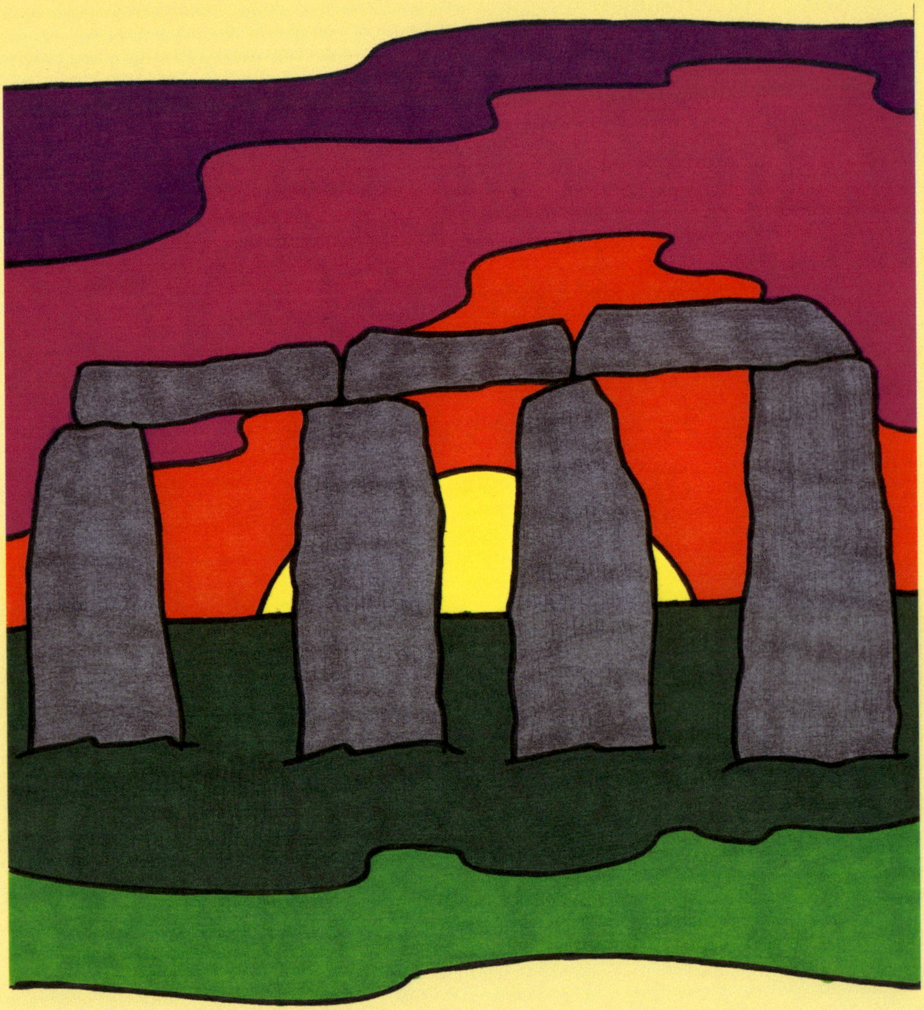

The Standing Stones

Along the megalithic pathway,
Trots the suburban fox,
Oblivious to the lunar phase,
And precession of the equinox.

Bright-eyed and bushy-tailed,
He's on a vulpine mission,
To avoid detection by the Druidic Grove,
Observing celestial transition.

Unreachable

Have compassion for the broken mind,
For inside of it we'll surely find,
The labyrinth of Theseus and his labours for birthright,
Draco's constricting embrace in the skies of the night,
Theta and delta waves of a nightmarish dream,
The neurotic expressionism of Munch's "The Scream".
Have compassion for the broken mind;
Please, please, please… be kind.

We Are One

The ocean heaves itself ashore,
Upon this watery sphere,
And in each and every drop of brine,
Does a hologram of the whole appear,
And as the spume becomes consumed,
In the next wave that breaks onshore,
So do we, eternally be,
Resorbed into the cosmic core.

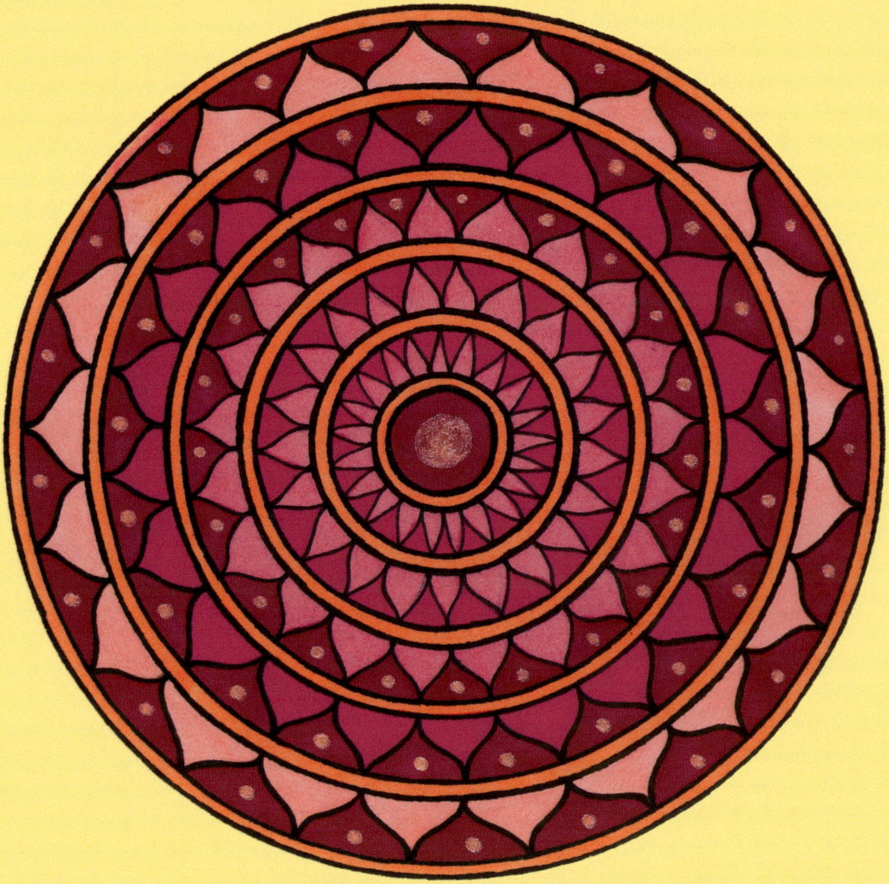

Chilling Out

Close your eyes and hold on tight,
For the incandescent festival of light;
For the rhythmic measure of the beating drum,
And to the hypnotic pulse, let your heart succumb.

Through the pounding of the Shaman's trip,
Experience the interdimensional slip.
Let rhythm and light be your guide;
Into the vortex, let yourself slide.

Magic and Mercury

The alchemist toils throughout the night,
In attempts to produce the pure, white light.
Hour after hour he works all alone,
The elements to transform into Philosopher's Stone.

The mission absorbs him and his life is on hold,
Until he can achieve transmutation of gold;
Yet his efforts produce nought but eternal strife,
And the feeling of failure for the rest of his life.

If only he were content with that which he had,
History would not record this good man as mad.

Earth Tonic

Please give me time to run barefoot,
On the soft, green mantle that enshrouds you,
And to gather the living jewels which bedeck,
Your meadows when spring equinox is due.

Please let me breathe the dizzying air,
Of celandine, sweet violet and feverfew,
And wrap me in your cloak of bliss,
That my waning energy I may renew.

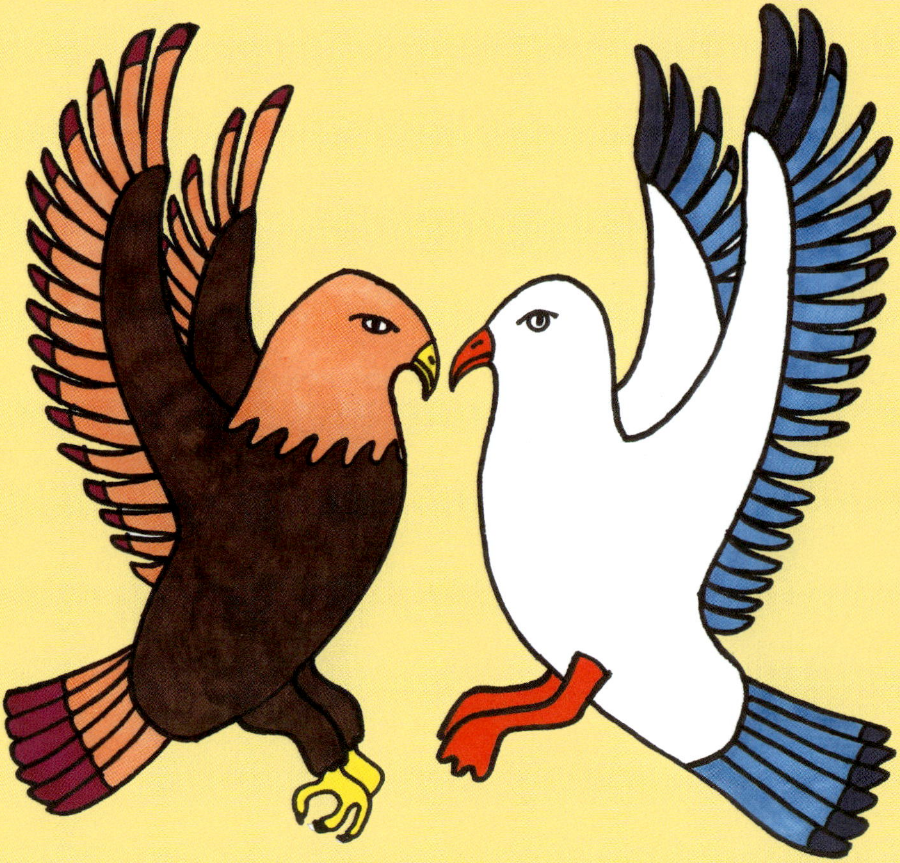

The Raptor and the Rascal

Soaring high, above mountainous peaks,
Spiralling thermals the golden eagle seeks,
And riding eddies above the ocean air,
The common gull glides without a care.

Both are masters of their domain,
As blustery heights they strive to maintain.
Both instinctively seem to know,
That by rising above, their spirits will grow.

So onward and upward they climb in the skies,
'til metamorphosis they both realise.
Their earthly physiques gain nothing from this,
But their spirits attain most heavenly bliss.

No longer the predator,
No longer the knave, Raptor
and rascal, Transformed
on sky wave.

Attitude of Gratitude

My day is blessed each time I see,
The garden birds look back at me,
And not fly off in frenzied fright,
At speeds approaching meteorite!

Timber

Think not that the rainforest cannot talk,
For the trees have a language all of their own,
And on approach of the lumberman's circular saw,
They sense the meaning of the rhythmic drone.

Their leaves issue forth an alchemical signal,
To their arboreal siblings round about,
But our Maker fashioned them no feet for to run;
So their fate is to fall, as the loggers wipeout.

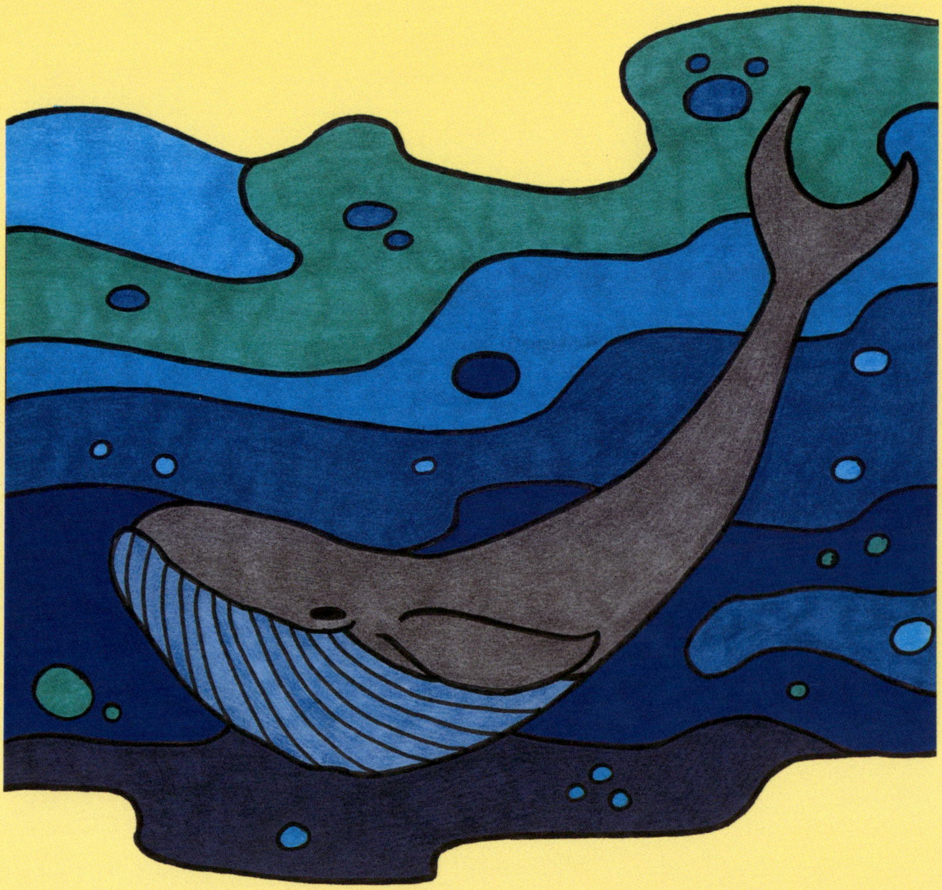

The Aristocracy

From the deepest depths of the ocean,
The stately cetaceans sing,
Their melancholic rhapsody,
With infrasonic ring.

Their elephantine frameworks,
Glide silently with ease,
Ladies of the ocean,
Lords of all the seas.

How can we fail to hear their cries,
To reduce our toxic blight?
Each year they beach upon our shores,
That we should note their plight.

Yet still the poison continues to be poured,
Straight into the homes of our Ladies and Lords.

A Nutty Situation

Prepare to leave your physics by the door,
As the grey-brown squirrel reaches out for more.
His feather-duster tail snakes in the wind,
As he suspends himself from just one claw.

His antics the birds seem to question,
Watching for the slightest suggestion,
That by hanging tail-up while feeding,
He'll soon back off with indigestion!

For Whom the Bell Tolls

As I watched the sunlight fade,
Over the windswept open moor,
A thousand pure white angels rode,
On horseback, as if to war.

They galloped across the rolling plain,
Dispersing to all corners,
Searching out all those in pain,
Paupers, misanthropes and mourners.

And whilst the afflicted bent in grief,
The angels ministered to their souls,
'til the light of dawn brought brief relief,
To those for whom the ominous bell tolls.

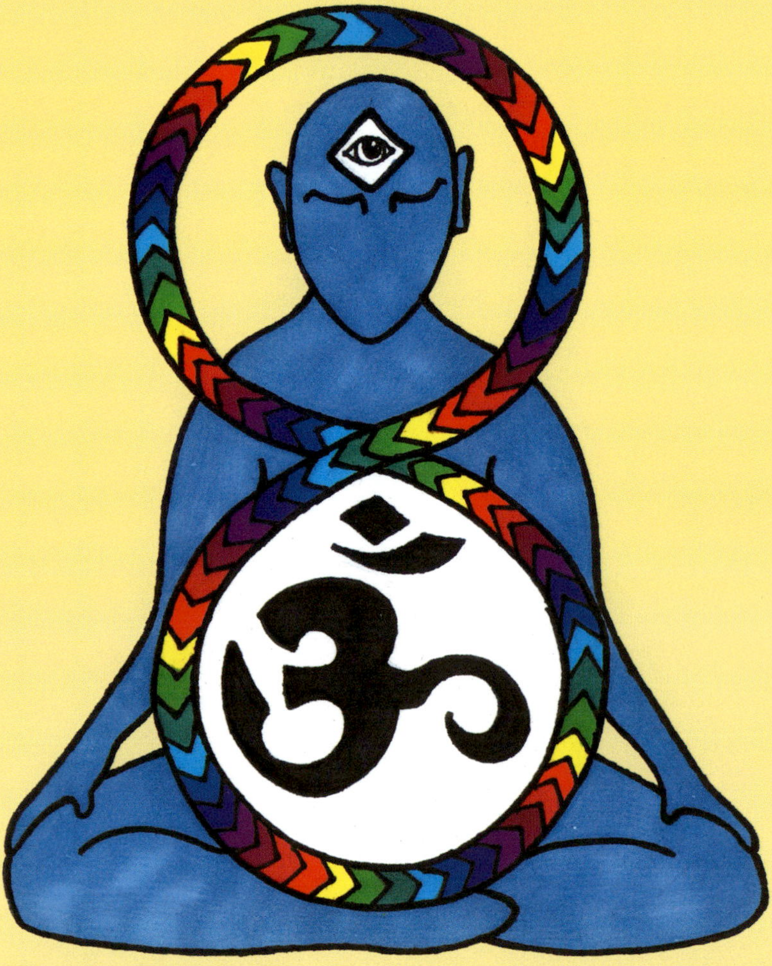

When All Else Fails

When Earth is trembling,
And the skies are heavy and dark;
When Man is erring,
And the watchdog has failed to bark;
When life is ebbing from the cradle of creation,
And hope is slipping,
Of any timely salvation…

Then where do we look,
To gladden our eyes?
How do we placate,
The mournful cries?

By looking within,
To the beating heart;
To the voice of the Universe,
Of which we're an infinite part;
The holographic matrix,
Of all that could ever be…

The Grand Universal Designer,
Of you… and me.

Columba Palumbus

The wood pigeon sits hunched upon the fence,
Buffeted by the fierce wind from the East;
His feather ruff is all fluffed up,
And his dove-grey suit all wrinkled and creased;
His beady, amber eye looks quizzically about,
As he hunkers down, preparing to sit it out.

Symphony
Colour 3 in Scarlet Major

Take to your allotted seats please,
For the Rhapsody in Two,
Followed by the Purple Overture,
And ending with Beethoven's Blue.

Then watch the golden eight go down,
Over the forest of aquamarine,
And pour yourself a seven,
Before leaving to catch the last green.

Our world vibrates with colour,
And the sacred numbers of creation;
But to see it all so clearly,
Requires a savant imagination.

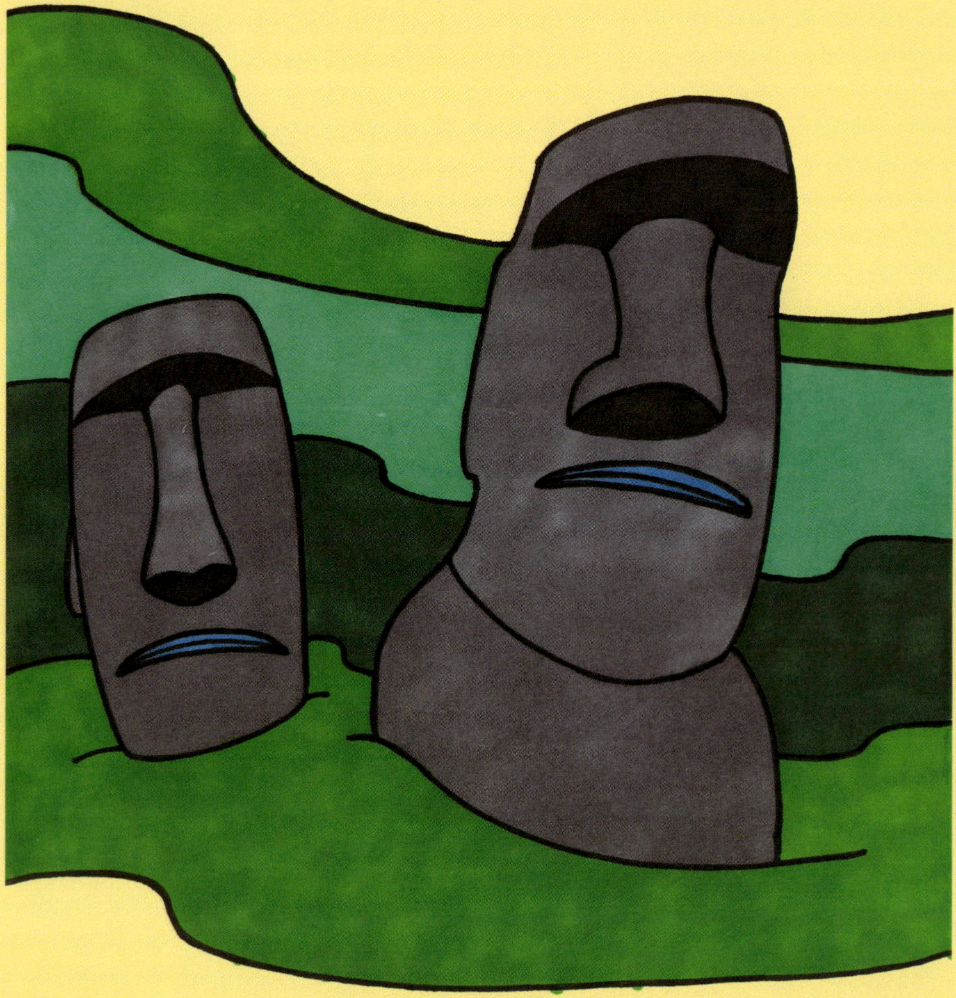

Rapa Nui

Tall and proud the statues stand,
Gazing out across the land.
The barren isle bears not one tree,
As the stoney faces stare out to sea.
For whose return are the petrified awaiting?
On what future prophecy are they speculating?

The Rocky Road

You, my friend, are not meant for this world;
The living is far too cruel.
Amidst the dregs of "civilisation",
You are a rare and splendid jewel.

I wish I could make your road smoother,
To let your heart sing and rejoice,
To unlock the chains of convention,
But the path you tread was your choice.

Knock Three Times

The stage is set and cameras placed;
On previous readings, their positions based.
The lights are off and the crew is braced;
With the metaphysical they wish to be faced.

The numinous Spirits gather all around,
Excited that their energies have been found.
Wishing no longer to be Earthbound,
Their desire to collaborate is profound.

When the investigation is started,
I do hope the dearly departed,
Are not too very downhearted,
When asked to "knock three times" ~ again!

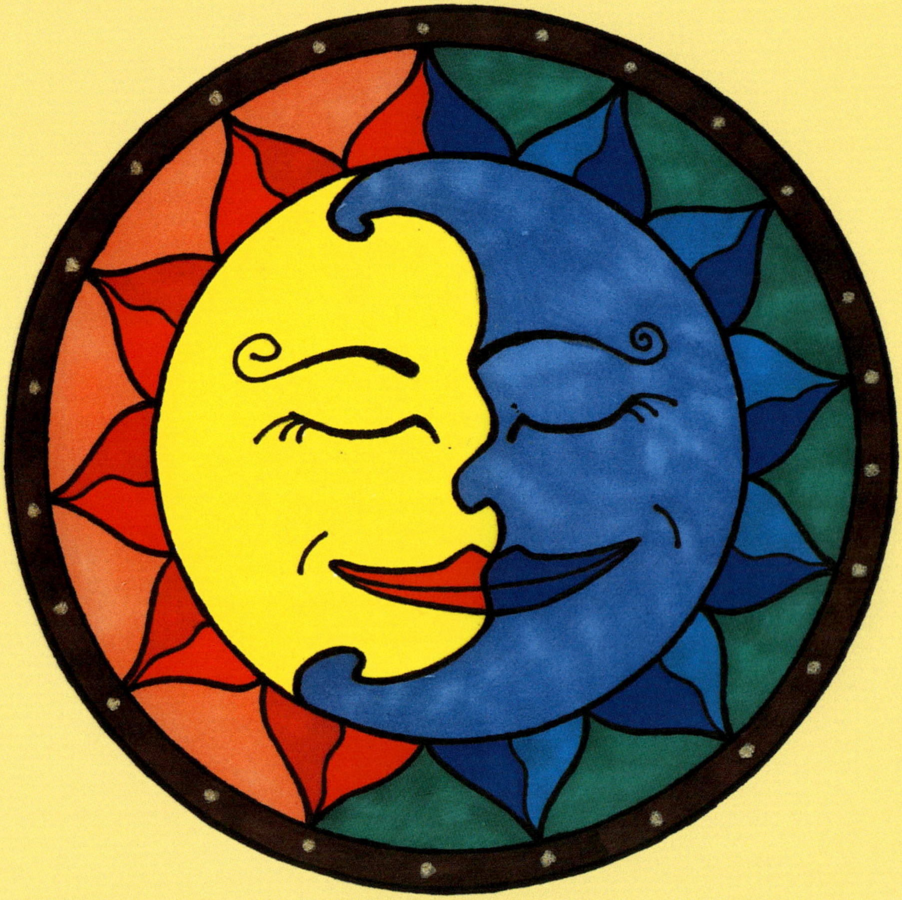

Walk This Way

If, while walking along your path,
You feel familiarity afoot,
Take care to seek the reason,
Why there you have been put.

For coincidence is but illusion,
Which leads to one conclusion:
You my friend are meant to be,
Walking on this path with me.

Thinking for Ourselves

Who said dark matter was just empty?
Who told us our DNA was junk?
Should we just accept the scientific view,
Or attempt, politely, these theories to debunk?

For our Universe is brimming,
With unlimited potential,
And with each passing day, our DNA,
Reveals itself to be essential.

Fleur-de-Lis

Defiant stand the flags of light,
Waving in the Summer breeze;
Pastel petals upon sturdy stems,
Declining the shade of any trees.

The rainbow goddess gave her name,
To these majestic flora;
And thus the Iris was crowned as queen,
With a halo fashioned by Aurora.

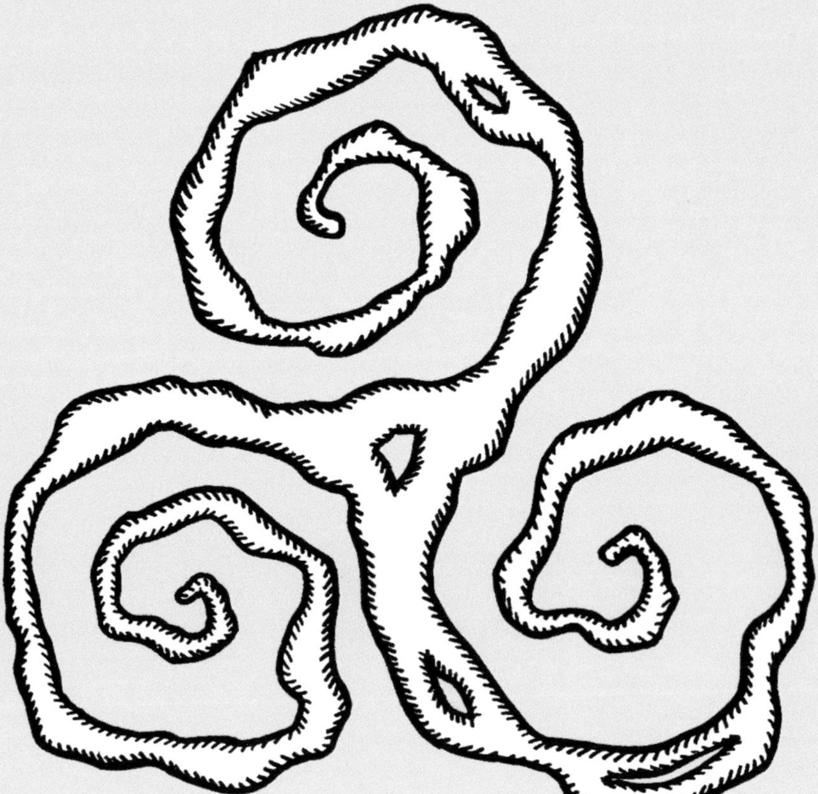

The Circle of Life

As the brooding clouds of Winter,
Give way to watery sun,
We dare to believe it's over,
And Springtime has begun.

The birds are gathering up the twigs,
The blossom is on the trees,
Fox cubs tumble on the lawn,
And there's none so busy as the bees.

Soon the lambs are all grown up,
And the roses are in full bloom,
Then the crops sway in the breeze,
And it's time for harvest to resume.

As the cotton clouds of Summer,
Give way to watery sun,
We fear it's nearly over,
And our time in the circle is done.

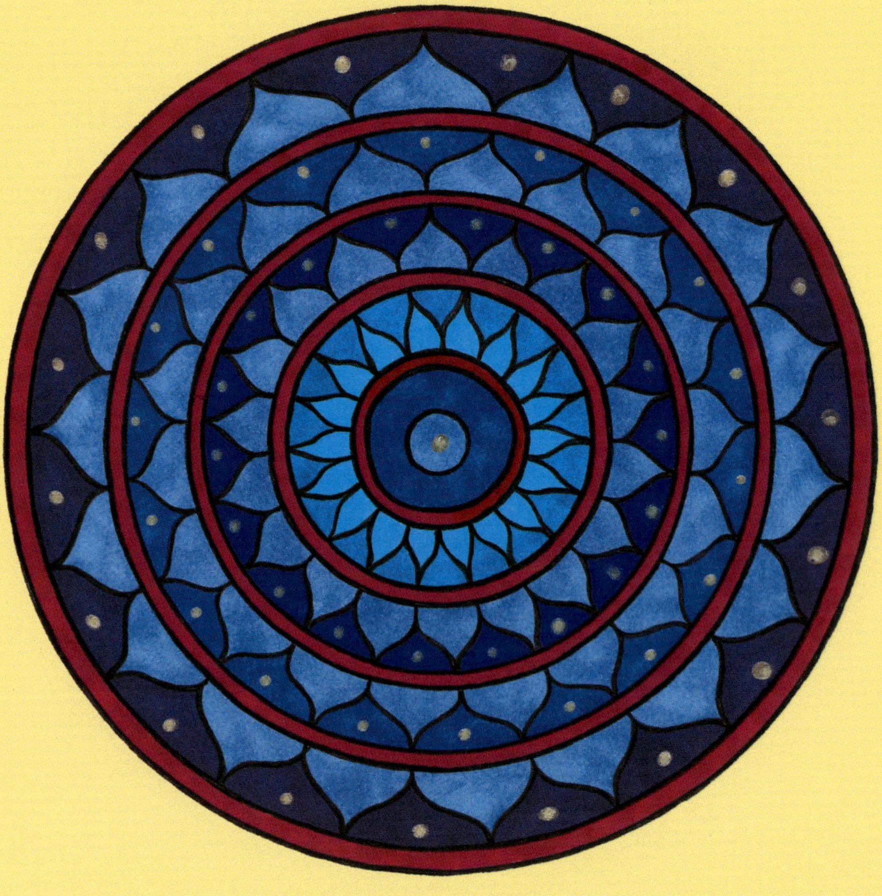

Home is
Where the Art is

The guided hand paints and draws;
It writes and weaves and sews.
There is no limit to its creation;
The guided hand just flows.

Every Second Counts

Time passes slowly for those who wait,
For those who watch and anticipate;
While for those who do, and gather, and sow,
Time passes swiftly, and before you know,
It's time to return to our Spirit form,
Where time is irrelevant,
But actions can transform.

You are a Star

When doubt creeps in to disturb your mind,
Don't let the darkness win.
Be brave, and seek to keep the faith;
Let belief in your Angelic Self begin.

You are a spark of cosmic divinity,
Sent here to expand your soul.
Your Eternal Self knows this is so,
And happily plays the role.

Try to recall that life is an illusion,
And keep the endgame in sight;
Stay true to your heart and play fairly,
To ensure your return to the light.

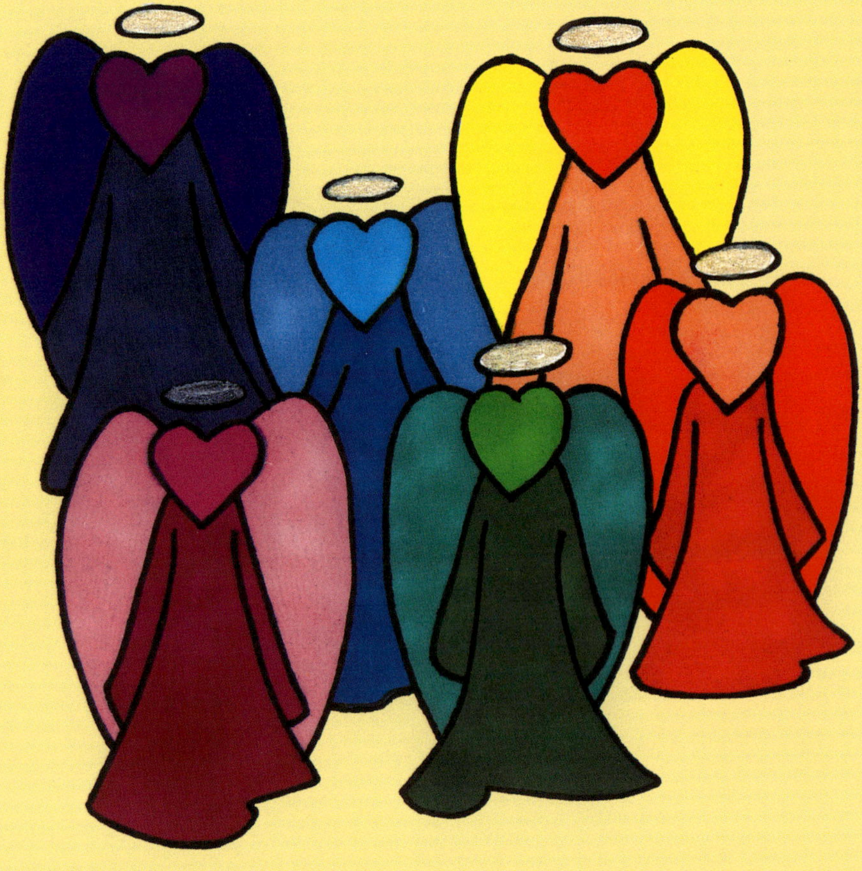

Angel Delight

The day God made the Angels,
Brightly shone the Sun;
He took the golden, solar rays,
Moulding each and every one…
Into Beings of such brilliance,
That none could look upon their form.
Their radiance was truly blinding;
And thus were the Celestial Orders born.

The day God made the Angels,
Sweetly sang the birds.
He took their ecstatic melodies,
Forming Angelic words…
Of such sweet and loving harmony,
Such clear and pure intent,
That all who hear their voices,
Will know whom God has sent.

So please thank the Angels every day,
For guiding us on our course,
And call on them to show the way,
Back to the One Eternal Source.

The House of Curved Light

Somewhere in the distant past,
There was a Golden Age of pride,
Where Gods and Men revered the Earth,
And her Laws of Nature were applied.

Whatever happened to that Golden Age,
That bright, rare beauty-spot?
Whatever happened to the land of love,
The place we all called Camu-lôt?

The
Living Landscape

How many drops in the ocean?
How many fish in the sea?
How many stones on the seashore?
How many leaves on a tree?

The ones who know the answer;
The ones who know its worth,
Are those who live in Nature:
The Devas of the Earth.

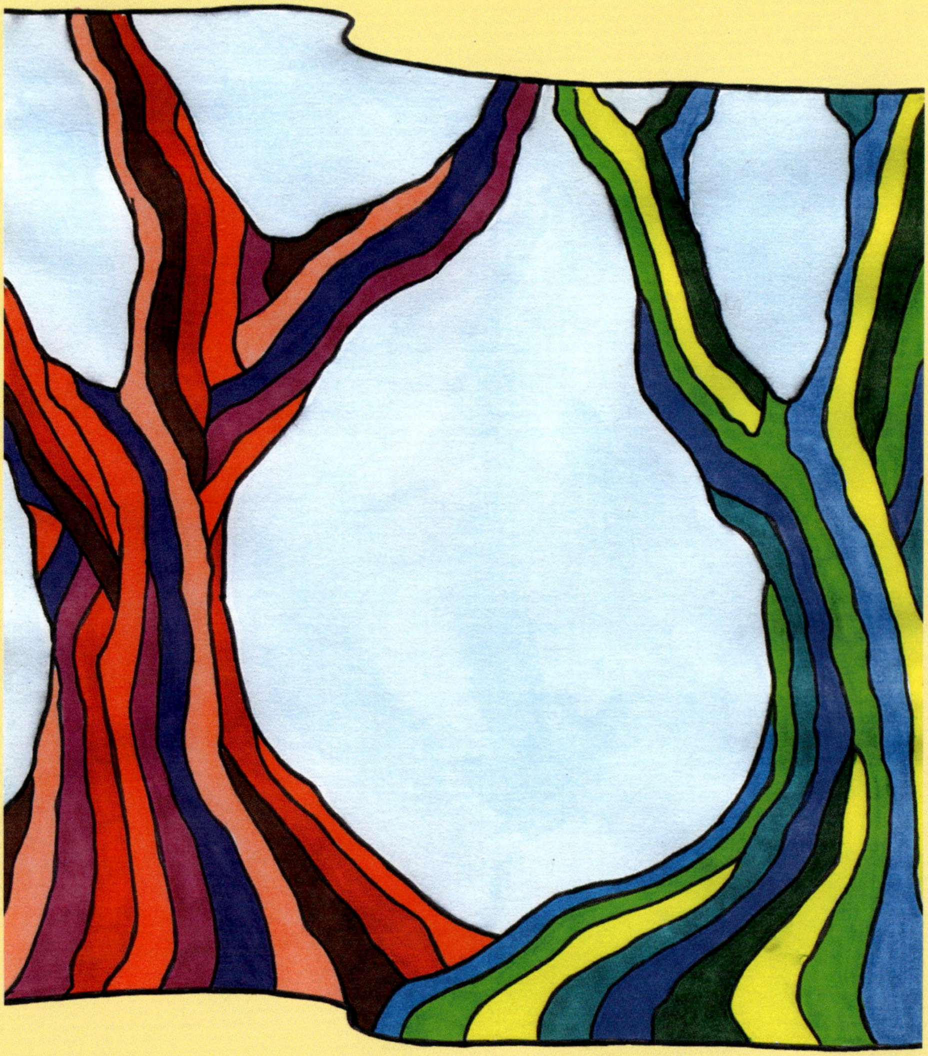

In Honour of Yew

Everlasting and evergreen it stands,
In myriad churchyards throughout the lands.

Proof of life eternal the Grand Designer has created,
But its limbs and boughs for bows were misappropriated.

The Sacred Yew has weathered all storms,
Witnessing many a beginning and end.

Lay down your bows; hate not your foes,
But embrace them as your friend.

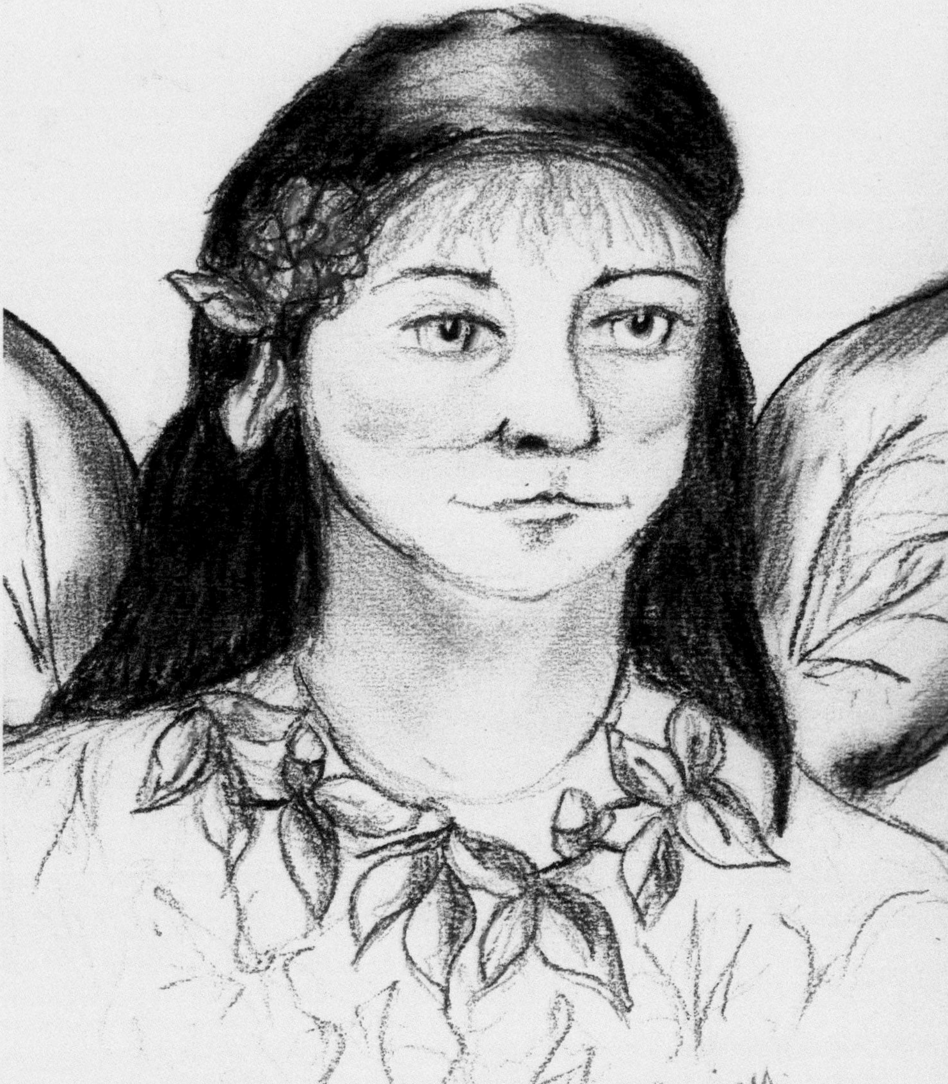
TATIANA
21/2/16

Titania

What right have they to say you don't exist;
That magic and miracles cannot ever be true;
That hopes and dreams are pure imagination;
That unicorns are just fantasy in their considered view?

What little faith and trust they have;
What lack of vision too.
I believe in fairies;
I believe in you.

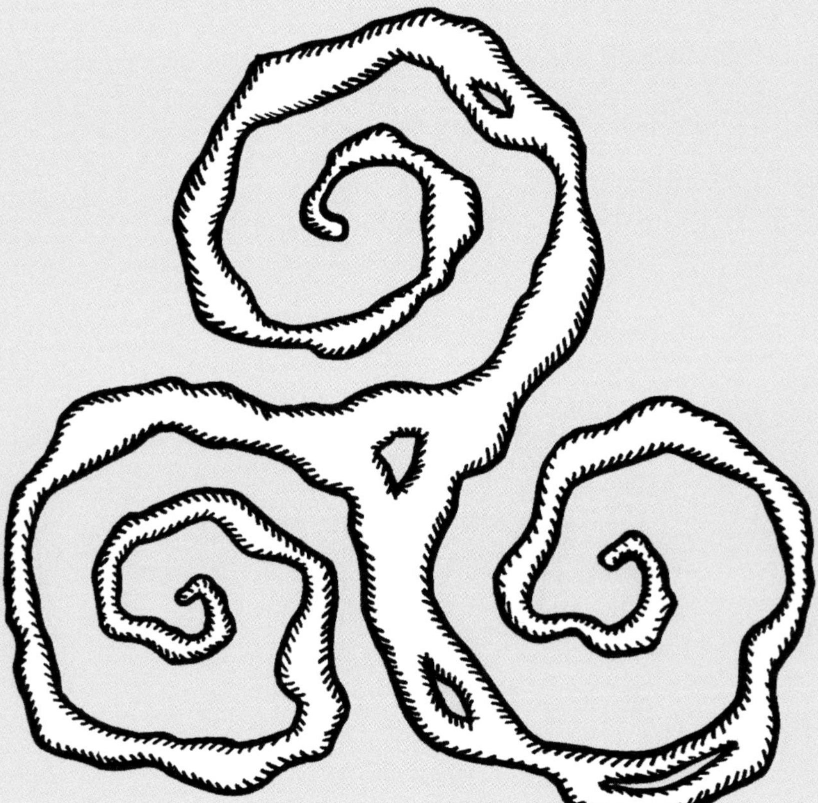

A Prayer for the World

Divine & glorious Earth, what handsome treasures do you conceal?
Your verdant pastures and luscious woods at Springtime will reveal…
The floral jewels of the Bride of May and all her retinue.
Each year the Earth displays this panoply of wealth anew.

Divine and glorious Earth, what plentiful sustenance do you supply?
The berries and the grains, the leaves, the roots, the myriad fungi.
The vines and nuts and petals too are all there for our taking;
Our cups truly overfloweth with the delicacies of your making.

Divine & glorious Earth, what deep & gentle healing do you provide?
Your pure spring wells, lakes & seas, your ocean & the countryside.
All these magical sanctuaries are there, free for us to use;
The calming waters and refreshing seas ~ all we need do is choose.

Divine & glorious Earth, what arcane and profound wisdom do you impart?
Your Natural Laws and Sacred Geometry speak directly to our heart.
The ebb and flow of oceans and the firefly's golden trail;
The hexagonal larder of the honeybee or the perfect spiral of a snail.

Divine and glorious Earth, what magic and mystery do you bestow?
The Angels of the heavens and the Elementals down below.
All are watching over us, to guide us each and every day;
Earth energies and leylines too will help us on our way.

Divine and glorious Earth, our waystation in this vast Universe;
You are our constant provider, our teacher and our nurse.
We give thanks for your bounty, your beauty and inspiration,
And we pray that your glory will reign forever over all of your Creation.

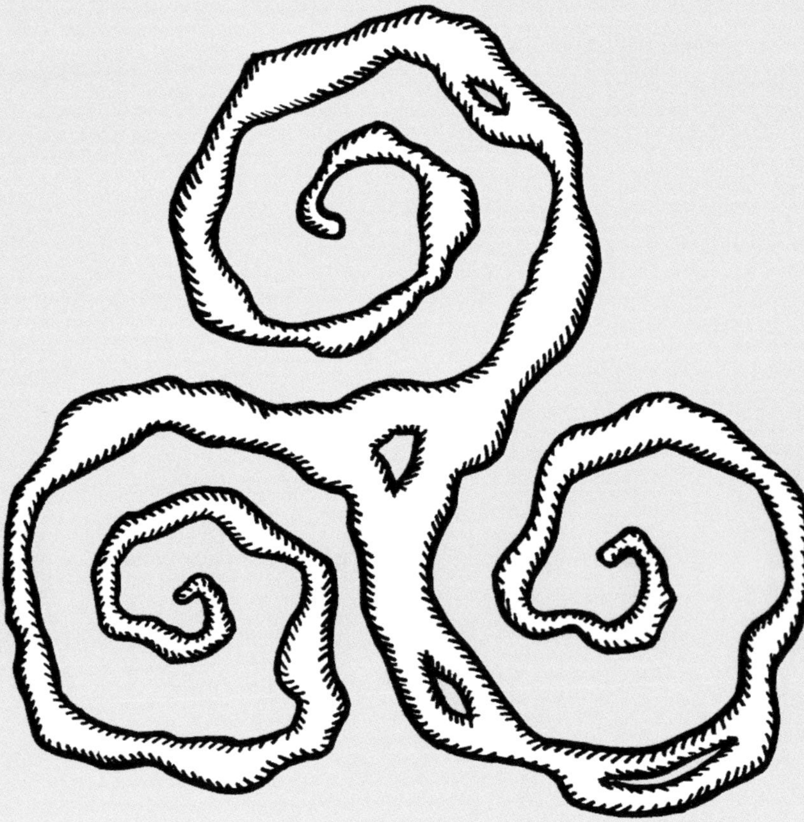

Going Home

To our guardians and angels we ought pray from birth;
Please hold our hands as we walk this Earth.
Guide us through life's labyrinthine path,
And lead us home to God's own hearth.

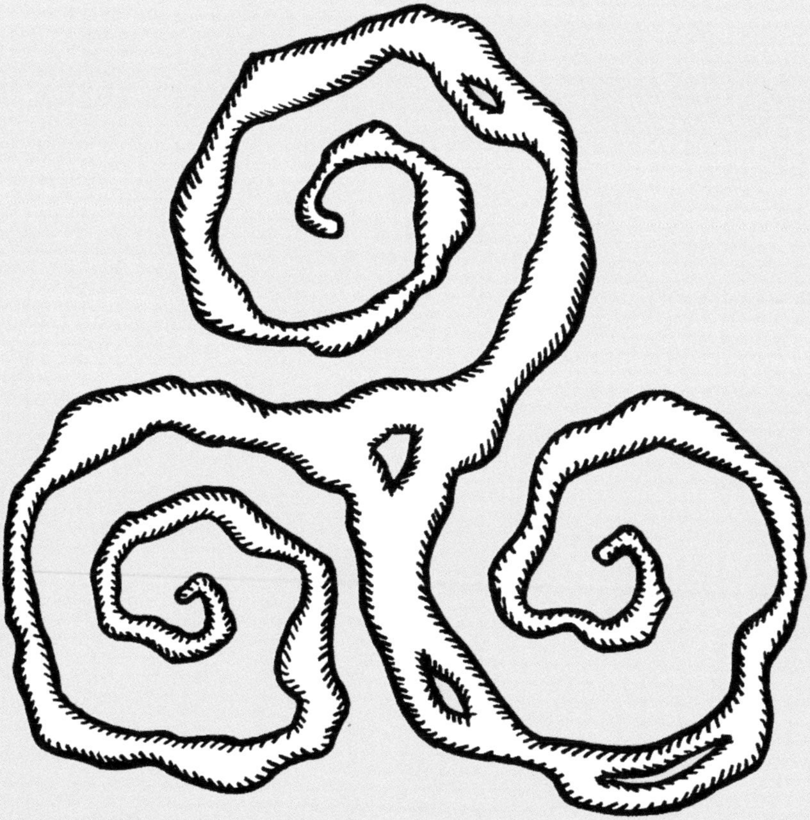